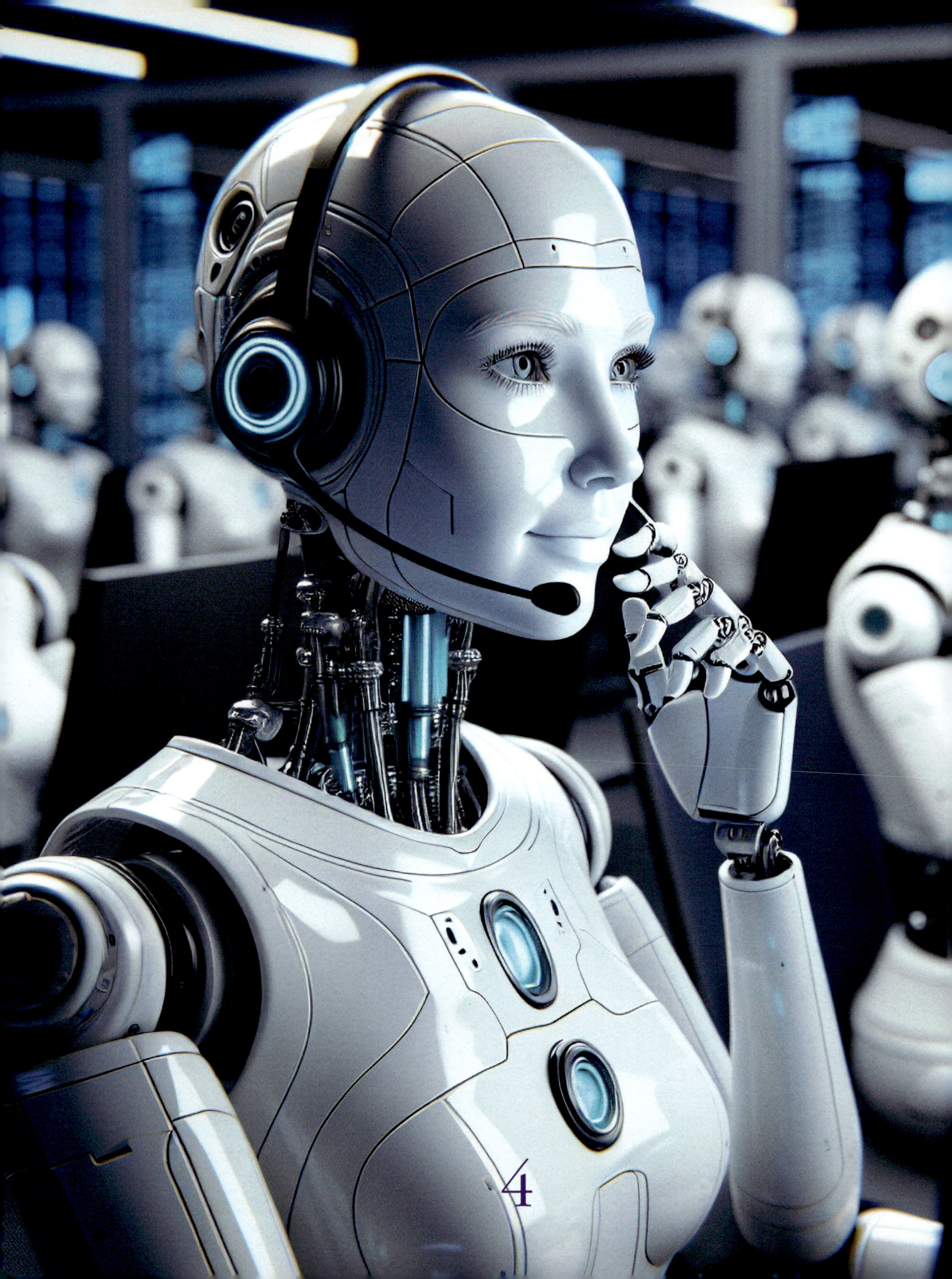
4

12 USES FOR ARTIFICIAL INTELLIGENCE IN BUSINESS

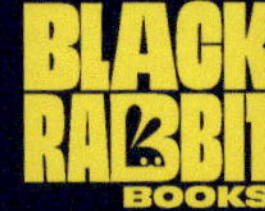

Table of Contents

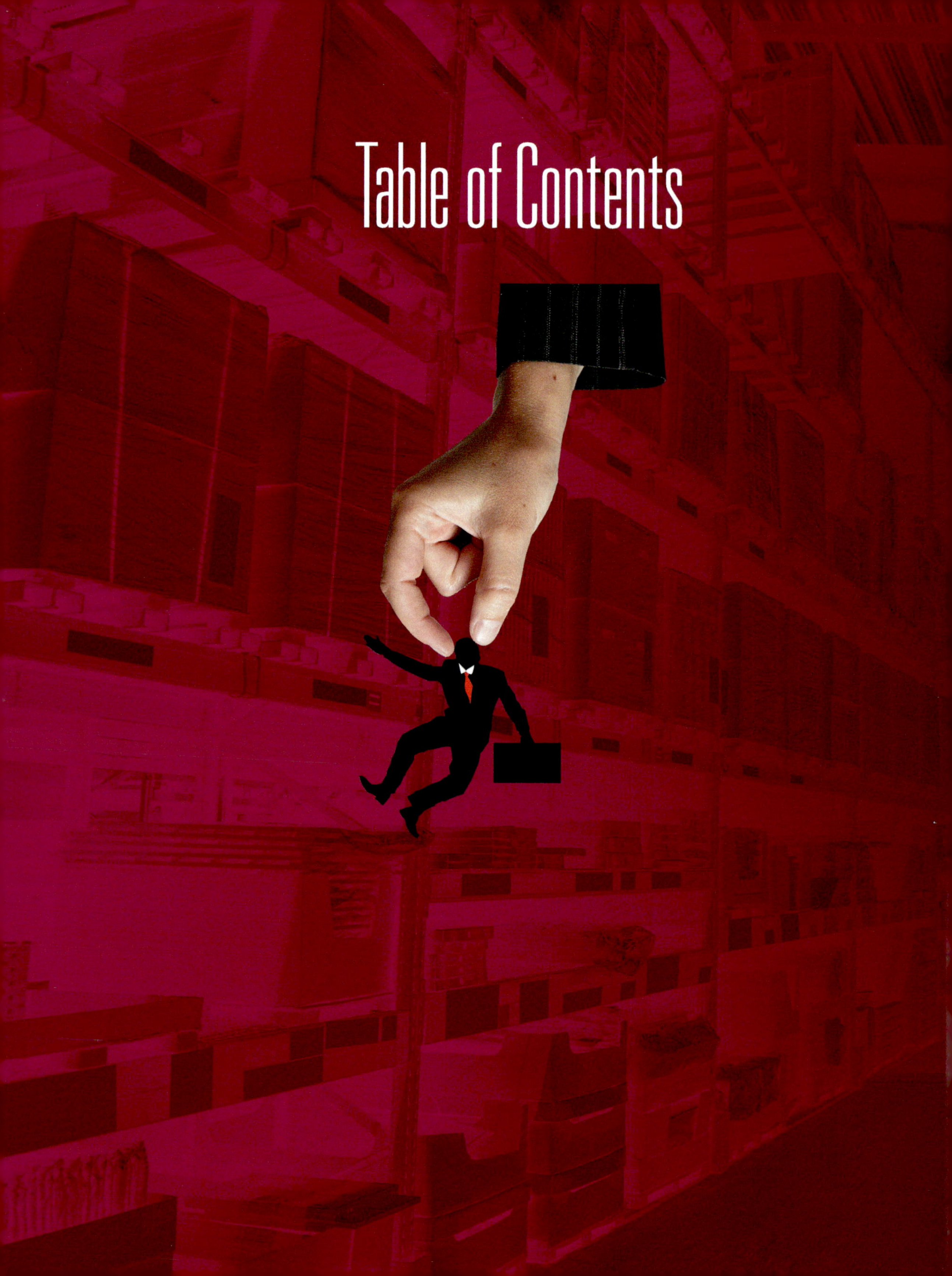

AI Changes
Call Centers
and Computers

Hello! Can you hear me? How can I help? Usually, customers with problems had to dial a phone number. It was for a call center. The caller might have to wait to talk to someone. They might have to explain their problem more than once.

Bad phone connections were annoying. An agent not understanding the problem could be frustrating. But a company called LivePerson uses **generative AI** to fix all of that.

LivePerson is a voice agent. When people call in, LivePerson is the first to answer. It has a lifelike voice. It knows when to stop and listen. It sounds as though it cares. It can even be customized with different accents.

LivePerson recognizes common problems. It finds solutions. If it can't find the answer, it sends the caller to a human. Some people have a hard time speaking on the phone. They can ask to move to texts or a messenger service. LivePerson can also send links, reminders, and instructions.

Using AI can take the strain off people who work in call centers too. Sometimes, customers are angry or frustrated. They take it out on call center agents. Letting a bot talk to customers first can help remove some of that stress.

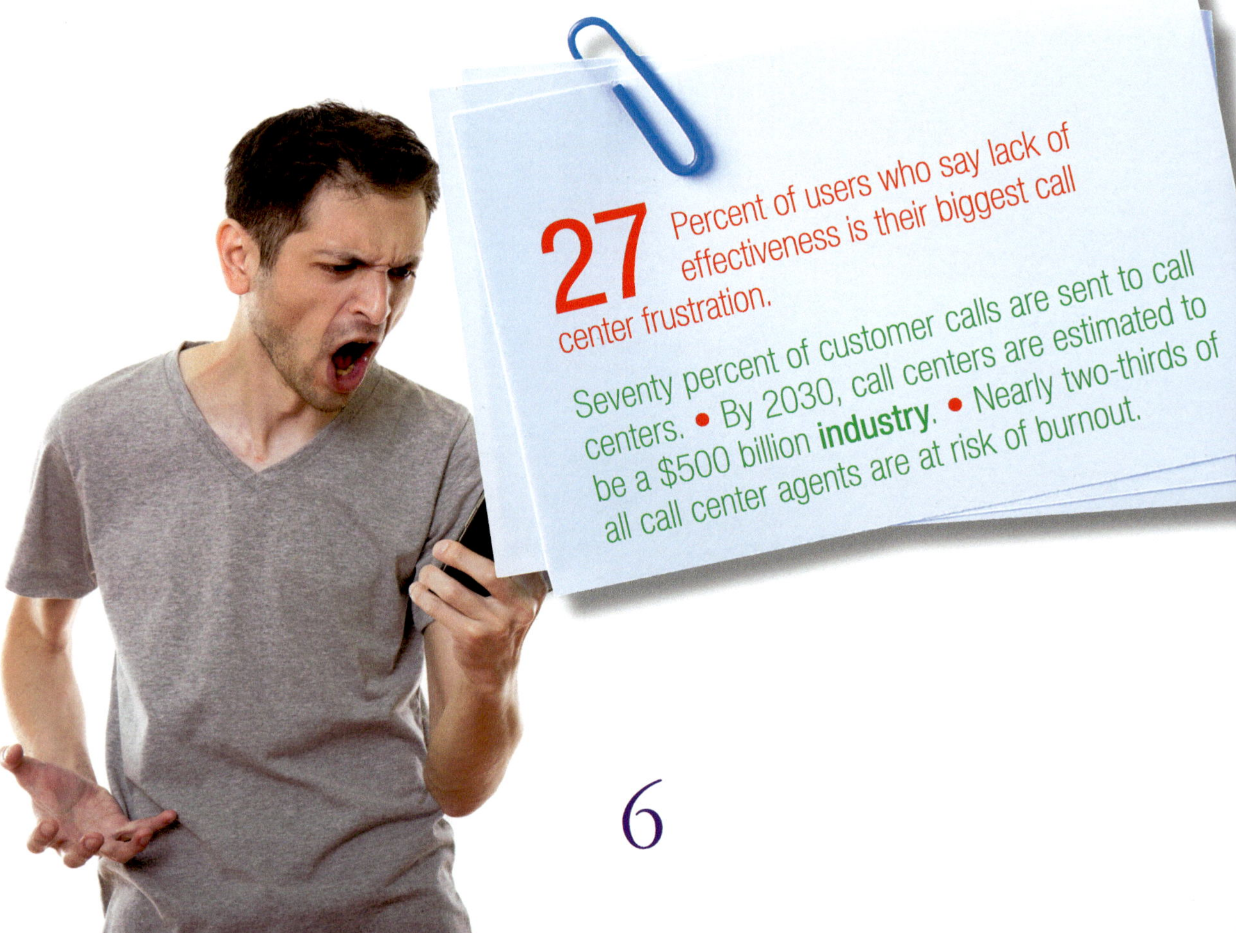

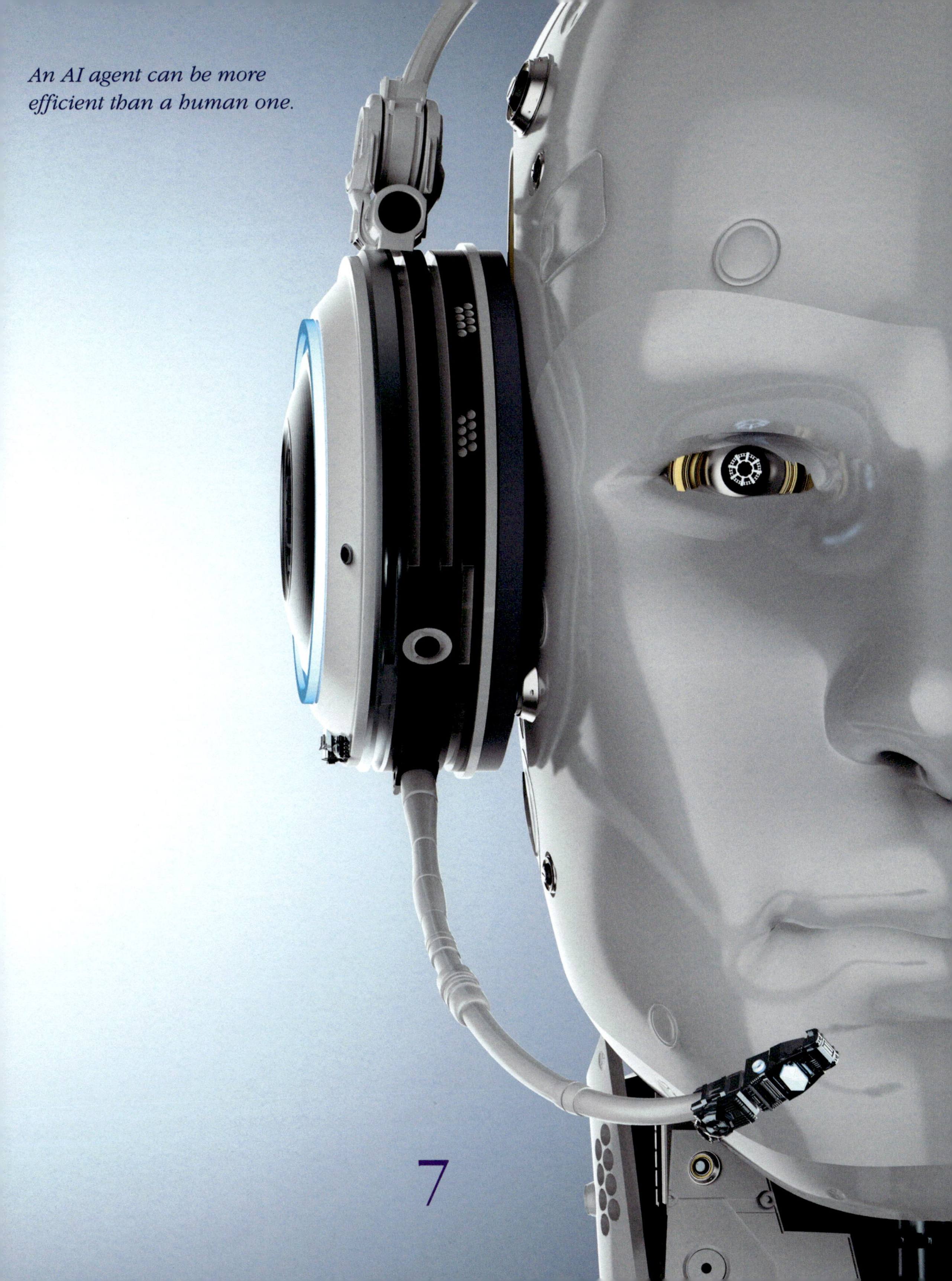

7

AI Helps Streaming *Pick Shows*

2

In 2024, more than 300 million people used the **streaming** service Netflix. Its library of titles changes all the time. It can be hard to pick what to watch next. It can also be hard to find new content. That's where AI comes in.

More than 80 percent of the shows on Netflix are chosen for viewers through personal recommendations. If you liked one show, Netflix suggests a similar one.

Netflix's AI **algorithm** logs how long people spend watching. It records if they marked it with a thumbs-up or a thumbs-down. It also tracks what time people watch. It sees where they stream from. It notes how many episodes they watch at once.

Netflix has a recommendation tab. It shows viewers shots from that movie or show. But they are not

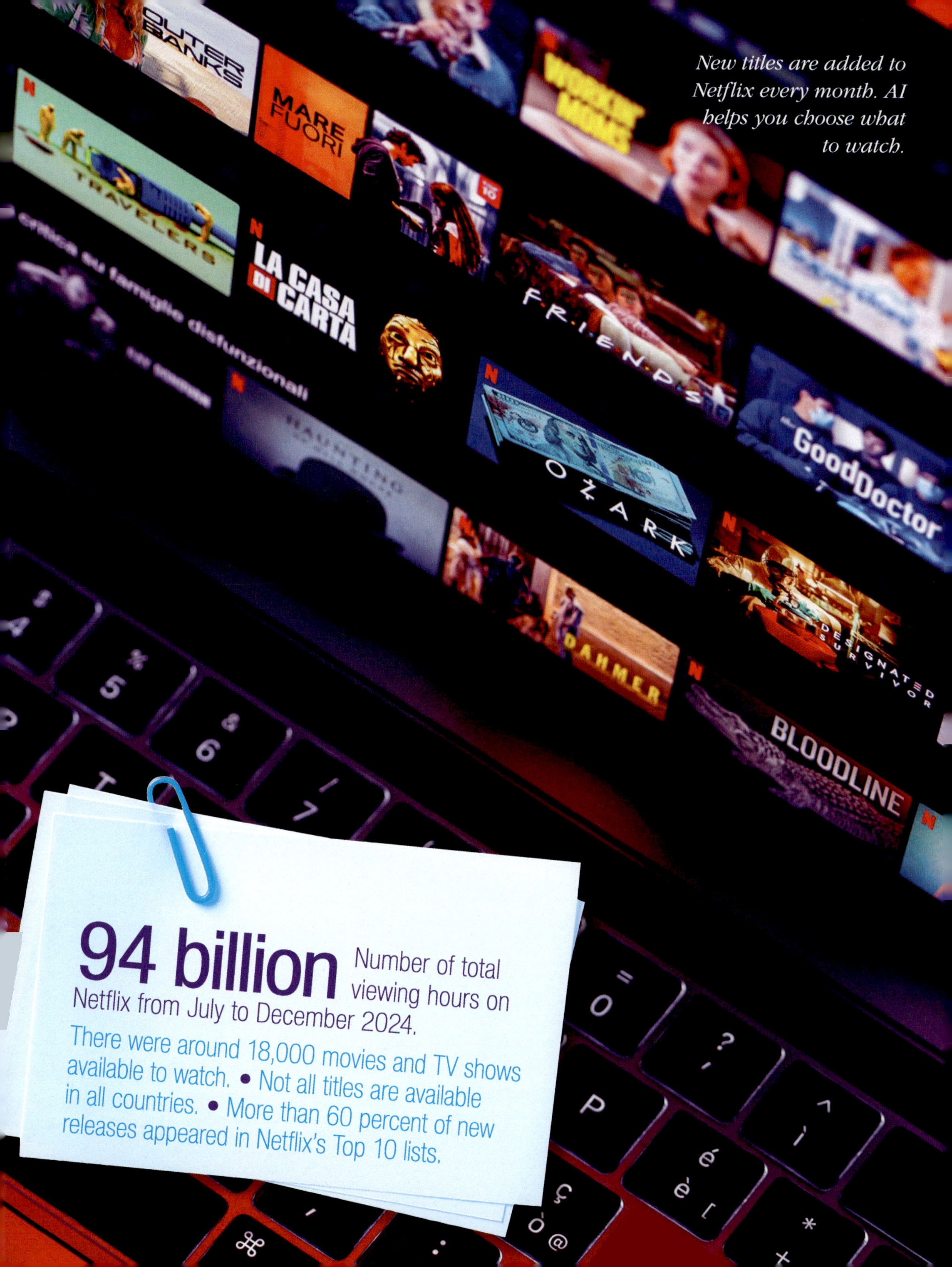

94 billion Number of total viewing hours on Netflix from July to December 2024.

There were around 18,000 movies and TV shows available to watch. • Not all titles are available in all countries. • More than 60 percent of new releases appeared in Netflix's Top 10 lists.

random images. AI has chosen them. It uses what it knows about the viewer. It picks what they find most interesting. The image may show a certain actor. It might show an exciting moment.

For example, a viewer might like sci-fi. Their image for a certain show could be of aliens or UFOs. The same image for a thriller fan could be of the alien doing something scary. But they would both be for the same show.

Can you think of other times where images are tailored to appeal to different people?

10

AI Takes Your *Order*

In 2023, the coffee company Starbucks made a vow. They would lean into **automation** and AI. They hoped it would bring in more younger customers. They showed something new. It had been in the works for years. It was an AI **platform** called Deep Brew.

Deep Brew works with Internet of Things (IoT) technology. Devices that have sensors, software, and internet access are part of the IoT. This means all smart devices are part of the IoT. Deep Brew uses the IoT to plan when machines will need fixing. It can also re-order supplies on its own. It schedules employees to come in during busy times.

People see Deep Brew too. They place an order. Starbucks' smart menu recognizes their voice. It changes what is shown on the screen. People can

see their options to change their drinks. They can also see the price in real time.

Every time a customer visits, Deep Brew looks at their past orders. It suggests new drinks based on what they've had before. It also offers discounts. This encourages people to come back.

Showing people what they liked worked. Deep Brew made Starbucks' loyalty program grow. It had 34 million users by early 2024. That was a 13 percent increase over the past year.

THE TURING TEST

In 1950, computer scientist Alan Turing asked a question. It was, "Can machines think?" He made a test called the Turing Test. A human asked both a computer and a person questions. The computer won if the human could not tell who was answering.

AI Gets Personal *at Home*

4

In 2011, Amazon started working on a voice-controlled computer. Three years later, they introduced Alexa. She could answer questions. She could set reminders. She used smart technology to connect to other Amazon devices. But that was just the start.

In 2025, Alexa+ was born. This new Alexa uses generative AI. It offers a more **personalized** experience. Users can hold natural conversations with Alexa+. It is like talking with a friend.

Alexa+ also works with digital services and the IoT. Together, they can order groceries or make dinner plans. They can also control smart devices at home.

Talking to Alexa is especially helpful for older users. They feel like they have a friend with them. Alexa also helps them make phone calls and send texts to family.

Alexa uses AI to understand your voice and help with tasks.

600 million
devices worldwide in 2025. Number of Alexa

A mobile Alexa+ app lets users talk to Alexa on the go. • It costs $19.99 per month. It is free for Prime members. • Around 80 percent of people 65 and older said they felt less alone with Alexa.

People with disabilities take advantage of Alexa as well. Working with smart devices makes their lives easier. They can turn off lights or lock doors with a voice command. This gives them a sense of independence.

Alexa+ helps people finish tasks they might find annoying. If an appliance breaks, Alexa+ looks online. She can find a service provider online. She makes sure they are a real business. Then she will make an appointment. Once the task is done, she alerts the owner. The owner knows exactly what is going on.

SMART ASSISTANTS

Alexa is not the only smart assistant out there. Siri, Gemini, and Bixby are a few others. The first digital speech recognition tool came out in 1961. It was the IBM Shoebox. It could recognize 16 words and numbers. In 2022, Alexa had more than 100,000 known skills.

Businesses Use AI to Market *Their Products*

There are many things to find and buy online. How do businesses make sure their product stands out? Good descriptions get people's attention. If they like what they read, they click to learn more. They might even buy that thing right away. ChatGPT and other content-generating tools keep descriptions fun and fresh.

Writing is not everyone's strong suit. And different people like different things. ChatGPT can adjust to fit each individual person. It can send out emails about sales or new items. It changes the tone for a personalized experience. The customer feels like that item was made just for them. If they aren't interested, AI tries to figure out why. It might send them another email trying a different tone.

ChatGPT can look at the descriptions written by people as well. It finds any spelling and grammar errors. People also use AI for inspiration. **Prompts** like "Write an ad campaign around shoes and clouds" can create new ideas. ChatGPT and other AI can even make new images based on the prompt. Then it's up to the person to bring those ideas to life.

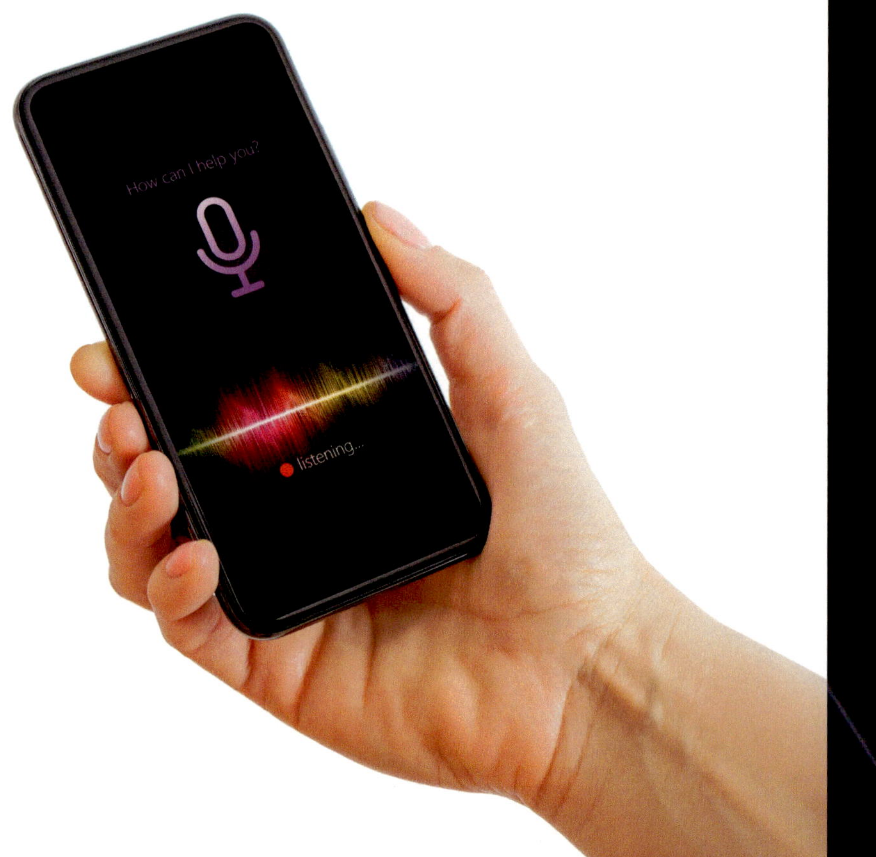

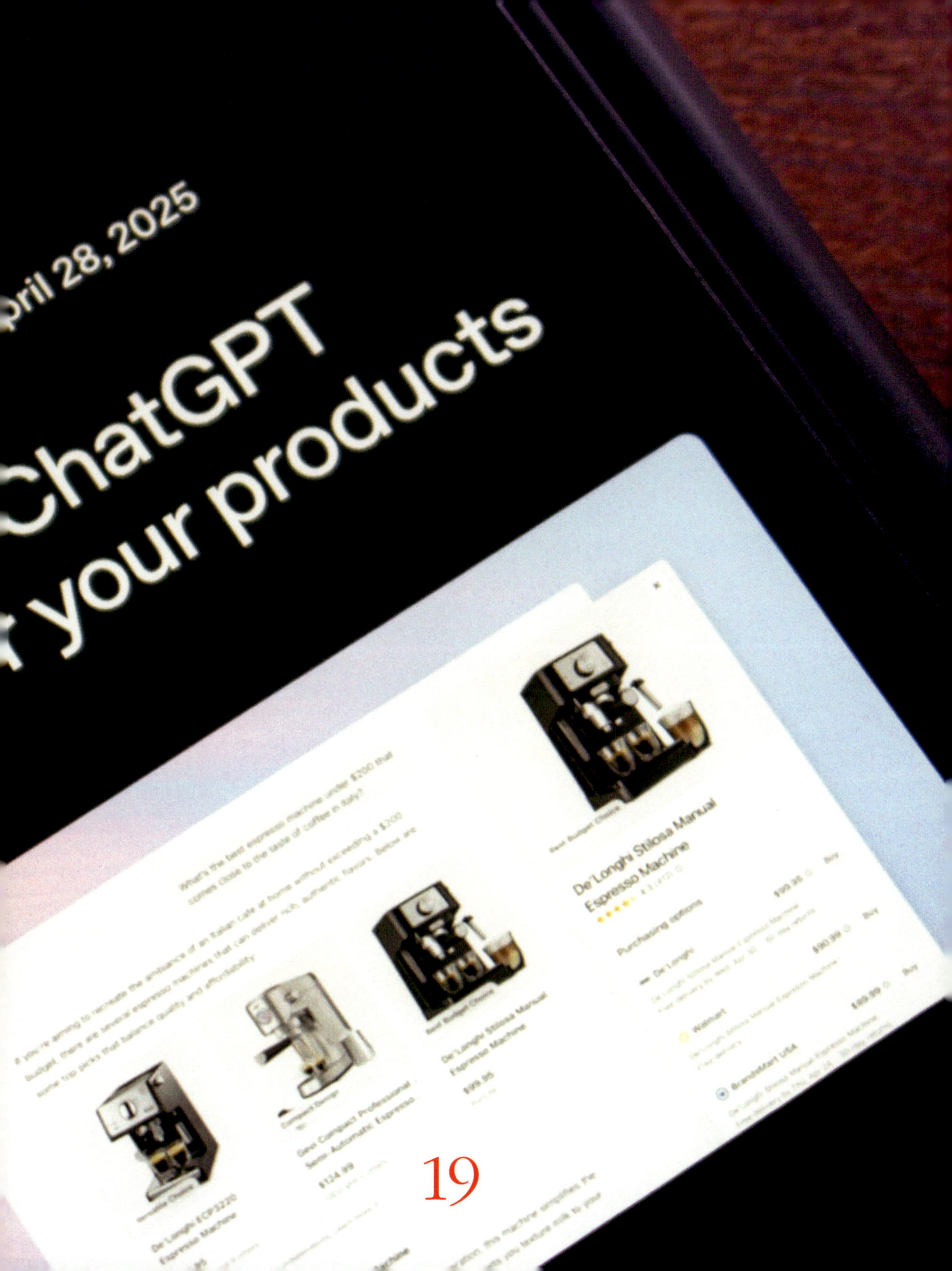

April 28, 2025

ChatGPT
your products

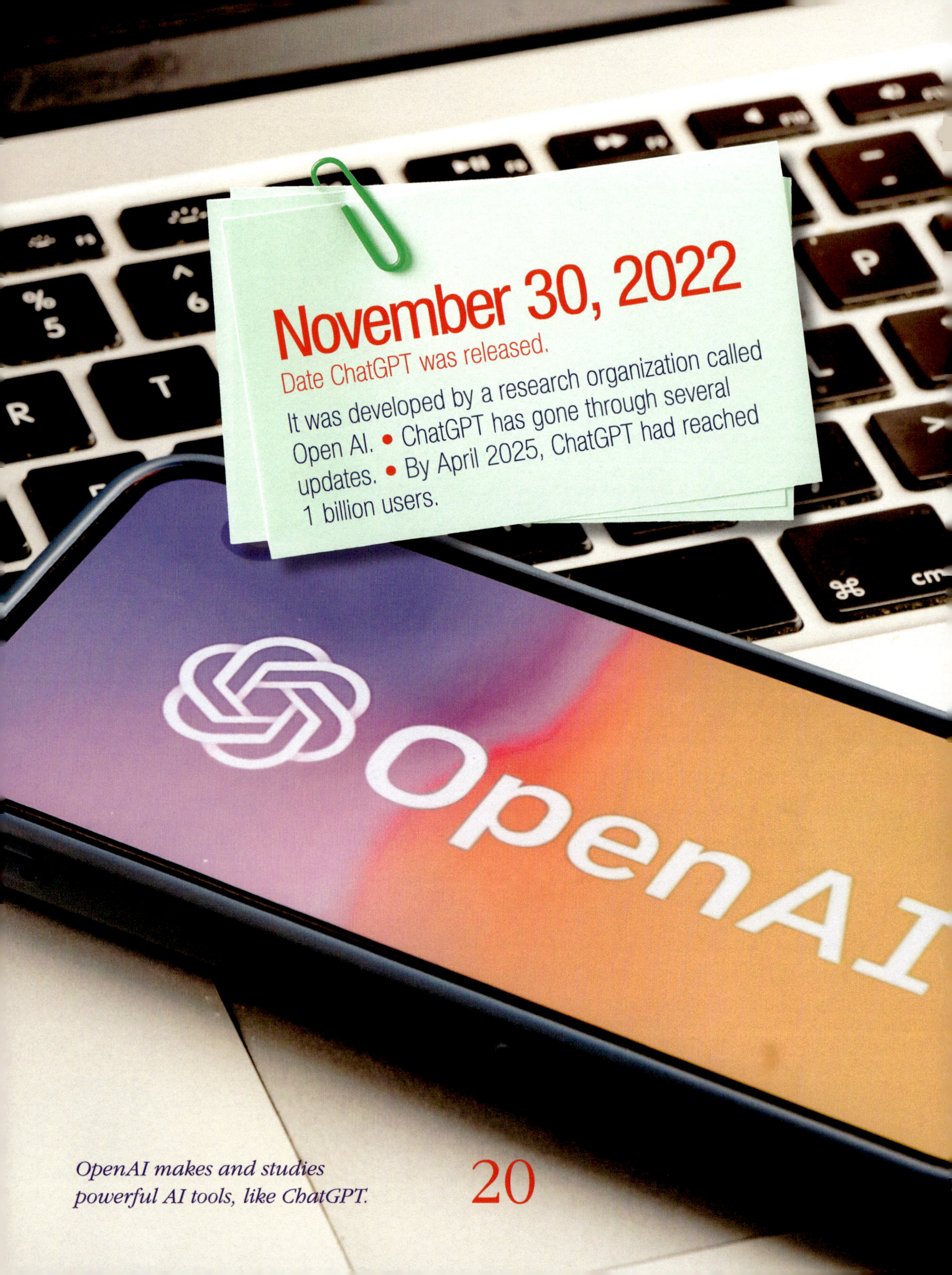

November 30, 2022

Date ChatGPT was released.

It was developed by a research organization called Open AI. • ChatGPT has gone through several updates. • By April 2025, ChatGPT had reached 1 billion users.

OpenAI makes and studies powerful AI tools, like ChatGPT.

AI Takes Interviews and *Helps Hire*

6

Finding the right person for a job takes a long time. Many people may want that job. They may all have similar skills. Hiring the wrong person can cost the company time and money. Using AI can help job **recruiters**. It looks at many people at once. This speeds things up.

Many jobs have keywords that match each job. Hiring managers usually look through papers that tell them about each person. These are called resumes. AI can review these papers, but much faster. It knows exactly what to look for. It can find the best person for the job.

Interviewing people is another step that can take a long time. AI can ask candidates specific questions. It compares answers to those given by current employees. It picks out people who sound like they would fit in well. And because the hiring manager has saved so much time, the person might be hired sooner.

AI does not usually have opinions on age, gender, race, or other personal details. Using AI to hire people could remove **bias** from the process. A human might have a negative experience with a certain school or a previous employer. They might automatically reject someone based on that bias. AI does not.

Think About It

Think about a bias you might have. Where does it come from? How does it change the way you feel about someone?

AI tools help employers sort through thousands of resumes.

5.5 million

Number of people in the United States hired at new jobs in 2024.

As of 2024, 88 percent of companies globally use AI to hire people. • Many companies spend nearly eight hours a week finding just one employee. • That time includes posting job openings online. They also look at resumes and interview people.

Robots and AI Get Packages *Shipped Faster*

7

Big companies store their products in warehouses. When something sells, an employee must find that item. They pick it off the shelves and scan it. Then they package and ship it. Keeping track of hundreds, or even thousands, of items is hard. Smart warehouses use AI. They make sure nothing ever runs out. They also make sure there is not too much of any one thing.

AI-powered **drones** inside warehouses look at **inventory**. They can travel in tight corners and through narrow hallways. They use GPS and **spatial** AI to know where they are at all times. They also have cameras and sensors. They use them to scan barcodes and product tags. They are connected to the IoT. This lets them share this information in real time.

Robotic arms are controlled with AI. They grasp objects and place them in the right-sized box.

In some warehouses, AI drones help track products and supplies.

4 million
Number of warehouse robots in 2025.

They work in 50,000 different warehouses. • Some of the largest are owned by Tesla, Amazon, and Target. • Multiple orders are picked at the same time. • AI can reduce potential errors. • Using robots instead of people can save on hard labor.

AI tells the robot if the item is delicate. If it is a weird size, AI helps to choose the correct box. Robot arms can work 24/7. They never get tired or need rest. Orders can be packed any time of the day. Extra robots can be stored when not in use. They can be brought out to work during busy times.

Warehouse robots speed up the sorting and shipping process.

Some A.I.R.

8

Nike makes some of the most popular shoes in the world. Everyone has different feet, though. Sixty percent of people say their shoes don't fit correctly. Nike realized that using a ruler to measure feet was outdated.

In 2019, they introduced Nike Fit. It used a smartphone camera. It scanned feet. It took 13 different measurements. It also made a 3D model of the foot. Its AI told customers which Nike shoe would fit best.

By 2024, Nike was using AI for an even more custom fit. The company worked with 13 athletes. Some ran track or played basketball. Others played football or tennis. They answered questions about their favorite shoes. They talked about who inspired them.

The athletes also explained what shoes meant to them. They talked about shoes as a form of personal expression. The answers were run through AI software. The AI came up with hundreds of design ideas. The Athlete Imagined Revolution (A.I.R.) team used those ideas. They made each athlete a special pair of shoes. The shoes were 3D printed. People came to see them at a special event. Nike A.I.R. showed how AI could start a project and people could finish it.

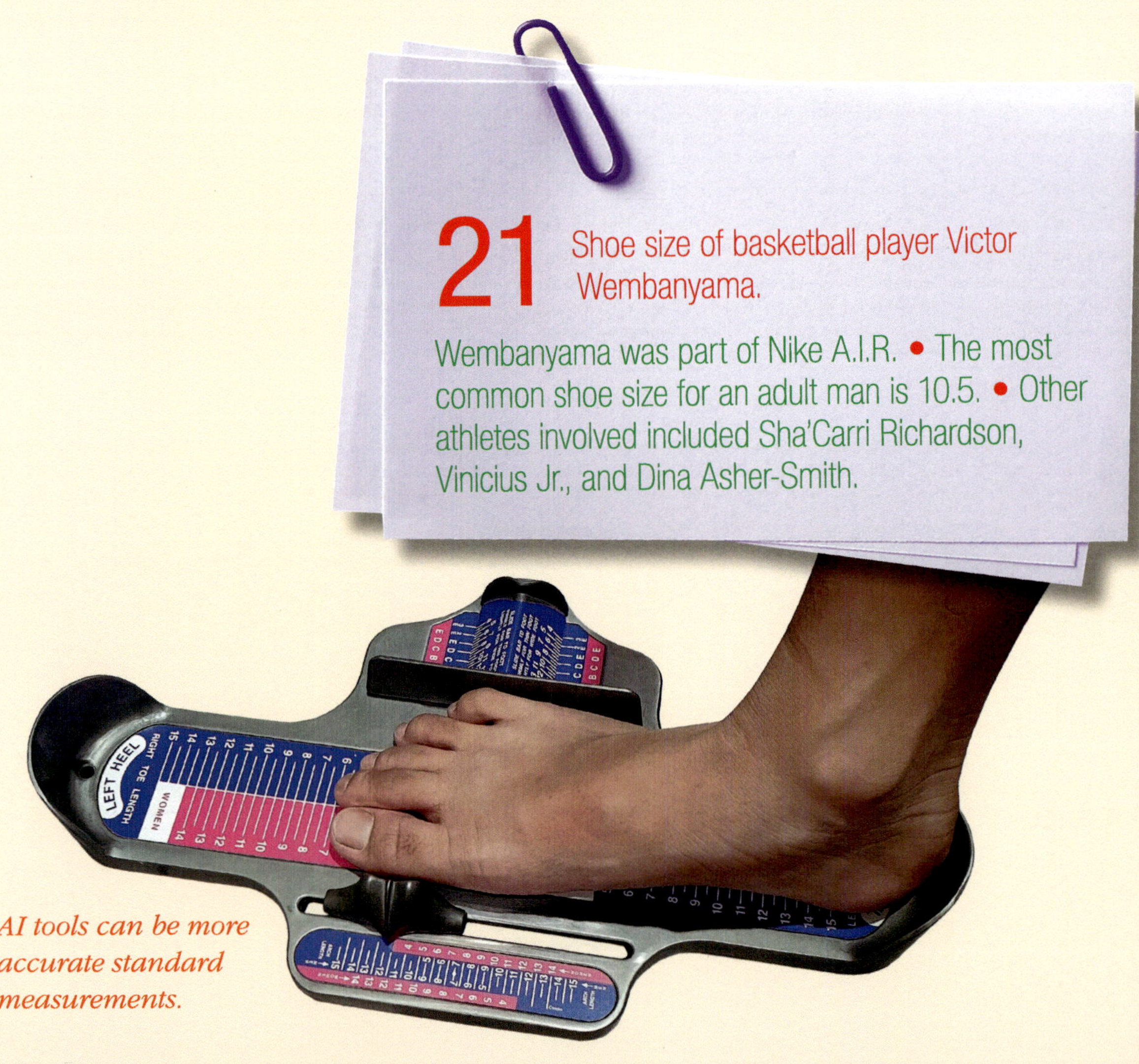

21 Shoe size of basketball player Victor Wembanyama.

Wembanyama was part of Nike A.I.R. • The most common shoe size for an adult man is 10.5. • Other athletes involved included Sha'Carri Richardson, Vinicius Jr., and Dina Asher-Smith.

AI tools can be more accurate standard measurements.

Think About It
Try designing your own
sneaker. How would you
express yourself through
your shoes? How could AI
help you with your idea?

29

AI Helps Engineer the Next Generation of *Plant-Based Food*

9

Food companies are always looking for ways to show off new products. Sometimes it is a limited-edition flavor. Other times, it is a partnership with an athlete or famous person. And sometimes, new items are part of a trend.

In 2022, Kraft Cheese noticed that plant-based foods were popular. But Kraft is a dairy company. How could they get in on the action?

Kraft partnered with NotCo. They are a plant-based food company in Chile. NotCo had an AI engine called Giuseppe. It had learned about thousands of plants. It understood them on a scientific level.

That knowledge was shared with food scientists. They listened to the AI's suggestions. They tried out new ingredient blends. Some more unusual blends included pineapple, cabbage, and beets.

With NotCo's AI, Kraft came up with new products.
They were made from plants. But they still looked like
popular Kraft foods. Their vegan cheese slices were
made with coconut oil, chickpea protein, and modified
corn starch. They came in American, provolone, and
cheddar flavors. They quickly became the best-selling
plant-based cheese slices in America.

Cheese wasn't the end of it. Kraft also made vegan
mayonnaise. Kraft mac and cheese and "NotDogs"
were close behind.

Think About It What's your favorite food? Would you try a vegan version? AI can
help you find new recipes. It can suggest vegan alternatives based on what you like.

42 Pounds (19 kilograms) of cheese the average American eats every year.
Cheese is a $258 billion business worldwide. • In 2023, 62 percent of US households bought plant-based products. • Vegans do not eat or use animal products. They eat plant-based products instead.

AI helps make plant-based foods that taste great and are healthy.

Using AI to Find the *Right Fit*

10

Have you ever looked for the perfect outfit but could never find it? In 2025, Google introduced a new AI image feature. Shoppers could create and shop for their own look. Users used Vision Match to describe their perfect item of clothing. Then AI suggested ideas. Users also found the best matches online.

Another Google feature used generative AI. It showed shoppers how clothing might fit them. Searching for a specific item would bring up the actual photos taken by that brand. Next, Google used AI to put that item on different people. They all had different skin tones and body types. This helped shoppers make decisions.

Google's AI also helped companies create new images without grabbing a camera. They could upload images from a previous ad campaign. The original images would tell AI about the company's brand identity. Then

34

Google's AI can help
pick the perfect outfit.

they could add an inspiration image and a prompt. Google would create a new image. It was similar to the original. But it had the new details added. This saved companies time and money. They didn't have to hire models or have photo shoots for new products.

SEEING STYLE Other companies are using ChatGPT or other chatbots to create virtual stylists. One early version let users scan their face and bodies. The stylist suggested the perfect outfit for each day. It even looked at the calendar and watched the weather.

Agriculture and AI Feed *the World*

Agriculture feeds the world. Farmers and ranchers raise our food. Every year, there are more people. But the amount of available farmland stays the same. Climate change and labor shortages make it harder to predict the future of farming too. AI can help agriculture become more streamlined.

John Deere makes farm machinery. They sell a driverless tractor. A person can drive it. But it usually drives by itself! The farmer can watch the tractor's progress on a smartphone or tablet. If the tractor senses a problem, it sends an alert. The farmer can watch a live video feed.

The tractor uses 16 cameras to see its surroundings. AI helps decide whether the path the cameras see is a good one. The tractor knows when to break up soil or when to turn around. The farmer is free to do other tasks while it works. Autonomous tractors for corn and soybean farming are in the near future.

The tractor's camera can identify weeds. It tells the tractor when and where to spray herbicide. This has saved 66 percent in herbicide use. Using less herbicides is better for people and the planet. It also saves money.

Smart tractors use AI to plant and harvest crops.

39

Students See AI as the Future *of Business*

12

AI and business go hand-in-hand. Business students want to learn all they can about using AI. In 2024, two-thirds of employers are looking for graduates who are good at AI.

Some schools have started offering courses in AI. Students study how AI learns from data, called deep learning. They test out large language models. That's a type of AI that can understand and recreate human language. Students also learn about diffusion models. This is a type of generative AI. It takes in data. Then it uses what it has learn to make its own.

Other schools have introduced AI assistants. Students use them as study tool. Harvard Business School

uses a bot called ChatLTV. It knows the basics of the coursework. It can help students fully understand what they're learning. It is different from ChatGPT. ChatGPT makes up its own answers if it doesn't have the right one. If ChatLTV doesn't know, it won't answer.

There are business degrees that focus on AI. Students study computer science. They also study business topics, such as economics and finance. Graduates figure out how AI can streamline workflow. These skills can make a business better.

WRONG ANSWER

AI can be used to teach. It can also be used to stop cheating. Some schools ban chatbots. They want students to find the answers themselves. Others use tools that help them grade. The tools guess how likely it is that text was written by a student or AI.

16,000 Number of business schools around the world.

Business school students learn how to run companies. • Some graduates go on to earn a Master of Business Administration (MBA). • People who earn MBAs can earn more money at their jobs.

43

AI helps business students learn faster and solve real-world problems.

Fact

- A simple chatbot can be created as fast as a few weeks. However, the more intelligent the chatbot, the longer it will take to develop. OpenAI's GPT-4, which powers ChatGPT, is the most complex. The bot has been trained on trillions of units of data, called tokens.

- Mindtrip helps people decide where to take their next vacation. Travelers enter what they want to see or do. They describe how they like to travel. Friends and family can jump in. Mindtrip sends pictures, reviews, and interactive maps. It makes recommendations. It even helps them book flights and hotels.

Sheet

- Working as a team is an important part of most businesses. AI can automate schedules and assign tasks to make the work flow easier and faster. AI can create a summary of what was talked about in video calls. AI-powered platforms like MURAL let coworkers collaborate on ideas no matter where they are in the world.

- Constructing new buildings is expensive. It requires a lot of planning. AI planning tools such as Buildxact give estimates on cost and project needs. Its intuitive model catches overlooked tasks or items. This prevents expensive surprises later down the line.

Glossary

algorithm
A set of steps that are followed to complete a computer process.

automation
The method of making a device, a process, or a system operate by itself.

bias
A tendency to believe that some people or ideas are better than others that usually results in treating some people unfairly.

drone
An unmanned aircraft or ship guided by remote control or onboard computer.

generative AI
A form of artificial intelligence that produces text, images, and audio.

industry
A group of businesses that provide a particular product or service.

inventory
A complete list of items such as property, goods in stock, or the contents of a building.

personalized
To make personal.

platform
An application or website that serves as the base from which a service is provided.

prompt
A natural language text describing the task that an AI should perform.

recruiter
Somone who helps companies find and hire people for jobs.

spatial
Artificial intelligence systems that can understand and operate within 3D environments.

stream
A continuous flow of data sent to a computer over the internet.

For More Information

Books

Allen, John. *Exploring Careers in AI.* San Diego: ReferencePoint Press, Inc., 2025.

Crane, Cody. *What Is Artificial Intelligence?* New York: Scholastic Inc., 2025.

Ventura, Marne. *12 Questions about Artificial Intelligence.* Mankato, MN: Back Rabbit Books, 2026.

Websites

AI | Crash Course
thecrashcourse.com/topic/ai/

Artificial Intelligence (AI) | Britannica Kids
kids.britannica.com/students/article/artificial-intelligence-AI/272968

About the Author

Mari Bolte is a writer and editor who enjoys wondering about where the future of technology will take us. Whether it's exploring outer space or thinking about how AI can make her life easier, one might say she has her head in "the cloud."

Index

TOP RANK is published by Black Rabbit Books, P.O. Box 227, Mankato, MN, 56002. • Copyright © 2026 Black Rabbit Books. All rights reserved. No part of this book may be reproduced in any form without written permission from the publisher. • Edited by Ana Brauer • Designed by Danny Nanos • Photographs © Dreamstime/Jinyu1963, 12–13, Olga Khelmitskaya, 39, Stockr, 38; Freepik/Phonlamaistudio, 26; Getty Images/Christopher Furlong, 13, Lew Robertson, 30, Thomas Faull, 44, timandtim, 27; Shutterstock/AlinStock, 37, Andrey_Popov, 36, Belinda Pretorius, 48, bunny pixar, 21, Chaosamran_Studio, 41, DronG, 32–33, earthphotostock, 23, fizkes, 45, FlorianKunde, 31, FOTOKITA, 10, Ground Picture, 35, Grumpy Cow Studios, 15, Jolygon, 46–47, Kaspars Grinvalds, 18, khatib ragab, 17, Koshiro K, 19, LightField Studios, 34, LookerStudio, cover, 1, MacroEcon, 5, Maksym Dykha, 45, Mamun_Sheikh, 16, Mialcas, 29, NATA FUANGKAEW, 11, Phonlamai Photo, 7, Photo For Everything, 20, Ranta Images, 6, Ruggiero Scardigno, 8-9, Saidulm872, 10, Santiago Cornejo, 2, 22, Scharfsinn, 2-3, 24–25, Shutterstock AI Generator, 4, SkyroseStudio, 28, thirasap phaknara, 42-43, Valentyn Volkov, 11, VDB Photos, 14, Vladeep, 44, vovan, 40 • Printed in the United States of America.

Library of Congress Cataloging-in-Publication Data: Names: Bolte, Mari author | Title: 12 uses for artificial intelligence in business / by Mari Bolte. | Other titles: Twelve uses for artificial intelligence in business | Description: Mankato, MN: Top Rank, an imprint of Black Rabbit Books, [2026] | Series: AI in the world | Includes bibliographical references and index. | Audience: Ages 9–13 | Audience: Grades 4–6 | Identifiers: LCCN 2025021450 (print) | LCCN 2025021451 (ebook) | ISBN 9781645825142 library binding | ISBN 9781645825326 paperback | ISBN 9781645825500 ebook | Subjects: LCSH: Artificial intelligence—Business applications—Juvenile literature | Business—Data processing—Juvenile literature | LCGFT: Literature | Classification: LCC HF5548.2 .B647 2026 (print) | LCC HF5548.2 (ebook) | DDC 658/.05—dc23/eng/20250818 | LC record available at https://lccn.loc.gov/2025021450 | LC ebook record available at https://lccn.loc.gov/2025021451